A Collection of Poems, Memories, and Six-Month Gu...

MOVING BEYOND THE Rainbow Bridge

Your Journey to Healing after Losing Your Dog

JULIETA L. SMITH

House of Seven Literature

Published by House of Seven Literature LLC
Copyright © 2023 by Julieta L. Smith

ISBN 979-8-9881254-0-2 (paperback)
ISBN 979-8-9881254-1-9 (hardcover)
LCCN 2023906975

Printed in the United States of America. All rights reserved. No part of the contents and/or cover may be reproduced, stored or transmitted in whole or in any part, or in any form or by any means, electronic, mechanical photocopying, recording, scanning, or otherwise without prior written permission of copyright owner or publisher. It is illegal to copy this book, post it to a website, or distribute it by any other means without permission.

Julieta L. Smith asserts the moral right to identified as the author of this work.

First edition 2023

Editorial Advisor: Anna Krusinski
Book Illustration: Nate Myers
Foreword: Dr. Kerrwen Tanner, DVM
Introduction: Aubriel Cameron

Unless otherwise indicated, all Scripture quotations are taken from the *New Living Translation Version* of the Bible.

Scripture quotations marked NLT are taken from the *Holy Bible*, New Living Translation, copyright ©1996, 2004, 2015 by Tyndale House Foundation. Used by permission of Tyndale House Publishers, Carol Stream, Illinois 60188. All rights reserved.

To Chez,

A Yorkie unlike any other. Thank you for the lessons learned and joy given, and for loving me with all of your little heart.

I love you forever,
Mommy

Contents

Foreword by Dr. Kerrwen Tanner, DVM vii
Introduction by Aubriel Cameron ix
Acknowledgments xi
Preface xiii
Behind the Curtain: My Story, My Chez 1
The Journey: Beginning Your Journey to Moving beyond the Rainbow Bridge . . . 9
First Month 15
Second Month 27
Third Month 39
Fourth Month 49
Fifth Month 55
Sixth Month 67
Create, Collage, Collaborate 87
Your Healing Continues 91

(Insert a photo of your dog.)

Foreword
by Dr. Kerrwen Tanner, DVM

AS A SMALL ANIMAL VETERINARIAN, practicing for nearly twenty years, I have had the opportunity to connect with families and help them in their journey of taking care of their new fur baby. It is a fulfilling job which brings new beginnings every day, and unfortunately, sad endings. I have learned over the years that we (veterinarians) do not leave our cases at the hospital or office. Rather, we create such strong bonds with our clients and their pets that we mentally take the cases home with us, and we endlessly ponder over the fur babies, clients, the diagnoses, decisions made, and advice given.

It is a heartwarming and exciting experience to meet a new client and their pet for the first time, and to then create a bond that last for years. In fact, we actually become our clients' and pets' extended family members. We just don't receive an invitation to family holiday dinners. We are present when our clients welcome their new human baby additions to their families. We observe from afar as their children grow from toddlers to college graduates. And we are present to see a spry, young, energetic puppy grow into a seasoned dog.

It is a wonderful feeling to provide medical guidance to clients to help them understand their fur babies. Unfortunately, in life there is an end. And just like the joy we experience meeting a new fur baby and its parents, there is immense sadness and heartache that we feel when we must perform a euthanasia. From afar, one would think it becomes easier over time to see the loss of a pet, but the reality is that it does not and never will, especially when we have grown so close to the pet and its family. Specifically, with each euthanasia that we perform, there is a part of us which we lose during the process. Conclusively, we grieve with our clients.

Chez was a dog who was a perfect example of the grief that we experience when a pet dies. Although Chez was not euthanized, after his demise, there was a very dark cloud that hovered over our hospital for days. Chez was loved by every employee in the hospital. He was a little guy that had a presence about himself. He was a very reserved, relaxed, and easygoing dog. He also demanded attention to the point that I would sit him in my lap while I typed my medical notes. He would not move but would sit perfectly still in my lap and fall asleep. Also, whenever he came to the hospital to visit me, he was always in his traveling carrier, which was his safe haven. When Ms. Smith entered, she would have the carrier on her shoulder and would sit it on the counter. Chez would poke his head out as if he was saying hello to everybody. To this day, I have his picture over my computer, and I glance at him periodically. He really was a special guy, and he meant so much to a lot of people. Therefore, it is only right that Ms. Smith would pour her feelings and thoughts into this book.

The author's transparency and vulnerability, which is displayed in this book, reaches out to the reader. This book will touch people who are suffering from a recent loss, and it will provide an avenue to express their deepest emotions. Even though we each grieve in our own way, this book will be a good foundation to begin the process.

Introduction

by Aubriel Cameron

WHEN JULIETA APPROACHED ME ABOUT this book, about how it was born out of the journey toward healing after such a sudden and tragic loss of sweet little Chez, my heart was so deeply moved. Having had the privilege of welcoming that sweet boy and his dedicated mother into my life, this book signifies the impact that he has had on lives greater than those within the walls of his home.

As an owner of dogs, a professional dog-sitter, and moreover, a lover of dogs, I know that a loss of life hurts in a way that is hard to describe. The unconditional love, the boundless joy, and the unrestricted compassion that is shown by our beloved dog every day of their life makes their departure such a deep, lasting wound that can take much time and effort to heal. Within the pages of this book, Julieta displays an honorable level of vulnerability as she guides the reader through the process of unpacking, grieving, rejoicing, and mourning the end of life of their furry companion. This book signifies so much more than the poetry within it, more than prompts to help you think, and more than words put to paper. This book represents the author's pursuit of healing after loss; it allows you to step inside the heart of someone who loved their animal wholly and truly, helping to narrate many of the sentiments felt by those who have experienced this and have paw prints left on their heart forever.

As the reader goes through this book, they will find moments where the heaviness of the emotions being discussed and processed really weighs one down. This can only be explained as being a part of the process, allowing yourself the space to feel the deep sadness, to feel the hurt that comes along after they've gone. Throughout the pages, encouragement can be found with thoughtfully placed Scripture, endearing poetry, and multiple opportunities for the reader to personalize the experience by writing their own responses and adding photos of their beloved pet along the way.

For the many years our animal is in our life, we are their entire world. The sun rises and sets with us, in their eyes. We can only pray that they feel the love we hold for them also. This book gives the reader an opportunity to write an "open letter" to their departed pet, to pen the feelings and words of hurt, memory, love, and joy. And by the end of the book, a feeling of catharsis can be had. Knowing there has been deliberate effort toward processing what has happened, but also being able to revisit these pages and fortify yourself, and see how far you've come in your healing, is priceless.

To Julieta, I feel so blessed and so fortunate to have had so many meaningful, beautiful moments with you and Chez over the past years. His birthday party and his Christmas sweater visits are wonderful memories! Chez knew that when he arrived at my home, he would have a warm bed and even warmer arms to welcome him. The impact that such a tiny guy made on the hearts of my children, myself, and my husband is still somewhat beyond words. I think of you both fondly and often. For trusting me to care for and love the best boy, I thank you.

To sweet Chez, I still can't believe that the last time I saw you was goodbye. But I hope you know that your "castle" is still here, and you're still the visiting king of our hearts. Kali misses you. We miss you. Your mommy misses you, and we know you miss her, too. Thank you for your love, sweet boy.

Acknowledgments

DR. KERRWEN TANNER, DVM, you are a talented and highly skilled doctor who always accurately diagnosed Chez and offered solutions that were in Chez's best interest. Chez was comfortable with you, which made me trust more easily. Lastly, after Chez died, the time you spent explaining the medical events and answering my numerous questions, while assuring me that I did everything that I could do, confirmed that you are absolutely the best veterinarian on this side of the rainbow bridge.

Tee Rogers, Alli Gantt, and Aubriel Cameron, you ladies and your families cared for Chez beyond my expectations, such that you loved him as your own dog. You never declined requests to watch him while I traveled, and you gleefully shared stories about his stay with you and how he was the little king of your castles. To know that each of you loved him as if he were your family member warmed my heart more than you will ever imagine. Thank you.

Grace Desir (Queen Grace) and Joy Desir (Princess Joy), my beautiful and intelligent nieces, from the time you were each two years old, you loved Chez in spite of your initial fear of dogs. You danced with him, walked him, talked to him, read to him, wrote him stories, and gave him the nickname of Buddy. He loved you immensely, and it made him the happiest little dog ever. Thank you.

Preface

WELCOME TO YOUR HEALING JOURNEY. This book with guided journal is specifically for dog owners. It is a collection of memories, poems, letters, and journal prompts which is structured to help you walk through the first six months of healing after the loss of your beloved four-legged fur family member.

This healing journal was birthed from a year of emotions that I experienced after the unexpected loss of my dog, Chez. Chez was a blond, black, and brown purebred Yorkshire terrier (Yorkie). He weighed 7.2 pounds, and he had a docked tail—and a personality that filled every space that he entered. As I will share in the next chapter, he was an anomaly because he was a quiet Yorkie and communicated with his eyes. He was calm and laid-back, such that many referred to him as a chill little dog. Chez was as helpful as he was kind.

He was a little dog that I could instruct only once, and he would follow the instruction. So, on March 9, 2022, at 10:00 a.m., when I looked into his brown eyes and understood there was a problem, I never fathomed he would be pronounced deceased by 1:15 p.m. that same day. His unexpected and swift departure was beyond devastating, and for months, I grieved without any direction. Moreover, I did not know how to navigate the grieving process of losing my little guy, who had become my child, nor did I understand how that process was supposed to look. I wanted to speak to God, but I was so overwhelmed with hurt from losing Chez that I told Him (God) that I was not speaking to Him; not because I was angry but because I was sad. And because I could not find my way out of the sadness, sadness found a temporary home within me.

I knew that I could not linger in sadness, and I was told by a counselor that I was depressed. As such, I began to write about my feelings, and I authored poems, letters, and memories of him. My journaling transitioned me to a space of smiling more than crying at Chez's memory. I began to laugh at habits I still do, which I once did to accommodate Chez. Additionally, I realized that, at six months into my twelve-month healing journey, I had created a road map to healing for grieving dog owners. At six months, I laughed more than I cried when I remembered Chez, and I could converse with others without feeling overwhelmed with sadness. Most importantly, I had reestablished my conversations with God (He is very patient). Therefore, I knew that six months was the measured marker for the guided journaling within this book.

I invite you into my life with Chez. The poems, memories, and letters that I have selected to share in this book reveal some of my most vulnerable, transparent moments, and they have allowed me to be the most authentic with you. It is my hope that sharing my vulnerable moments will help you through your healing process. The memories and poems in this book may evoke emotions of sadness and laughter, but it is my hope that the words will urge you to think of your beloved fur baby and will encourage you to write your own memories, poems, and letters. The monthly journal prompts will gently guide you to do the work for your own healing. You will read that my poems are not professionally structured; this is because I am not a professional poet, yet they are all written from my heart to inspire you while enriching your life. I encourage you to write your own poems without inhibition or concern about structure, style, or correctness because they are a reflection of what is in your heart.

Lastly, this book is divinely created for you, the grieving dog owner. There has never been a dedicated space, structured in this format, for grieving dog owners until now. It is my wish that this book will help you find the laughs that you need, help you release your bottled tears, and journey out of the sadness or guilt that you may feel. May you move beyond the rainbow bridge, which your fur baby has crossed and is eagerly awaiting your reunion with them on the other side.

> When tomorrow starts without me, don't think we're far apart, for every time you think of me, I'm right here in your heart.
> —Author unknown

Behind the Curtain

My Story, My Chez

THE FOLLOWING PAGES PULL BACK the veil on my story with Chez. It is a vulnerable and transparent view into who he was, and the events on the day he crossed the rainbow bridge. Writing the events from that day still brings tears to my eyes, but thinking about him with a smile that warms my heart means more. I have accepted that March 9, 2022, 1:15 p.m., was his time. His assignment on this earth was complete because there is a time and a season for everything in this life.

> For everything there is a season, a time for every activity under heaven.
> A time to be born and a time to die. A time to plant and a time to harvest.
> A time to kill and a time to heal. A time to tear down and a time to build up.
> A time to cry and a time to laugh. A time to grieve and a time to dance.
> —Ecclesiastes 3:1–4 (NLT)

While driving to pick up Chez from his foster home in 2009, I never fathomed how much I would learn from him, how much I would love him and eventually grieve him. He would become my best friend, fur baby, confidant, travel buddy, sous-chef (I will explain), and movie partner. Chez was a purebred Yorkshire terrier (Yorkie). His hair color (Yorkies do not have fur) was blond, brown, and black. At nine weeks old, he could fit into the palm of my hand. Born on November 19, 2008, in a litter of eight, he was a foster puppy to a Missouri police officer because the state had determined that the breeders of Chez's parents could not continue breeding dogs. Therefore, Chez and his siblings were temporarily fostered in different homes until they could be rehomed with their forever families. Upon seeing his little face on the pet adoption's website, I instantly knew that Chez was the puppy for me.

Chez was an anomaly for a terrier breed because he was quiet. In fact, many people were surprised to learn that a dog resided in my home because they never heard him bark. However, Chez appropriated his moments to bark, which was always done for valid reasons. For example, when a houseguest removed their shoes, Chez would bark if their feet did not smell "fresh." Nothing a little sprinkle of baby powder wouldn't resolve. However, it still embarrassed me. I would attempt to distract him as I watched him sniff at a guest's toes. I'd brace myself as I watched his docked tail wiggle rapidly from side to side because I knew Chez was about to speak. With his head lowered, he would inhale swiftly, and then his back legs would kick back and outward, like a bull before it charges. Chez would raise his head and let out several short, high-pitched barks at the guest. He would then pause and wait for the guest to respond. If there was no response, he would bark again. The guest would sit confused. Without speaking, and silently apologizing, I would extend a bottle of baby powder toward the guest and request them to sprinkle a little inside of their socks. The guest's reaction of disbelief, and the statement, "I know he is not telling me my feet stink," was the guaranteed response. I sometimes shrugged to confirm their statement. Chez would monitor the situation by standing at a respectful distance from the foot-odor offender. After the guest applied the baby powder to their socks, Chez would return to inspect their work by sniffing their feet. Upon his satisfaction, he would walk away to show his approval. I often questioned Chez about his actions, but with time, I realized that human feet were in his airspace; therefore, it was his prerogative to inform the human of their odorous situation.

Chez also barked when people spoke loudly. With just he and I living in the house—in a quiet atmosphere—Chez relished in peace. Therefore, he promptly reminded humans to use their "inside" voices. These memories make me smile because he was a one-of-a-kind dog. So many people loved him, such that it made it easy to obtain a sitter. He received requests to sit for high school senior cap-and-gown photos (which he obliged), and he received credit for some families obtaining their own dogs. Yet I always warned the new pet family that their new dog would not have the personality, or be as well-mannered and trained as Chez; he was uniquely humanlike.

Chez's persona drew comments like, "He does not think that he is a dog," from many who encountered him. As such, I believed the comments were accurate because it was the two of us together for fourteen years, and I treated him like a real-life boy (nod to Pinocchio). I spoke to Chez as if he understood everything that was occurring in my life. Similarly, there were moments when I truly believed he did.

He was my travel buddy and accumulated more airline frequent flier miles and highway travel miles than the average dog. He relocated with me to three states and consoled me with the pat of his tiny paw when I was ill. And he was my sous-chef. When I prepared meals, Chez would sniff near the cooking range and would bark once when my food was ready to be removed from the oven. Ironically, he was always correct, and I never overbaked a meal during his watch.

Chez's long-term veterinarian, Dr. Tanner, referred to him as "my boy," and his staff showered him with affection and attention. Chez was a true ham because he relished in the affection and attention shown from others, such that even his trips to the vet included required routine acknowledgments from staff as they worked. Allow me to explain. Chez always arrived at the vet in his soft-side travel case with his little head poking out of the top of the bag's access. He loved being inside of his bag, and the staff understood to place him inside of their crate with his bag. However, Chez was not the little Yorkie to be ignored. As Dr. Tanner communicated to me during Chez's vet visits, every so often, he would poke his little head out of the opening of his travel bag and emit one high-pitched bark before silently waiting for acknowledgment. If he did not receive a response, he would emit a second high-pitched bark, at which time, one of the staff members or an attending doctor would reply, "Hey, Chez." Satisfied with the acknowledgment, Chez would retreat into his travel bag like a groundhog who had seen its shadow. He trained the doctors and staff well.

Chez was so intertwined in my life that I forgot that his life span—a dog's life span—was shorter than a human's. I bequeathed him in my will, as I did for my human family members, because Chez had become human to me—a fur human. He was a fur human who trained me to love with all that I have, give selflessly, forgive quickly, laugh loudly, and create emotional boundaries. Chez keenly sensed a person's spirit. And he was sometimes described as reserved and stoic when he was not feeling well. So, when Chez suddenly died at fourteen years old, it ripped out my heart, and I was left numb, dazed, and unable to process the events of his death.

On March 9, 2022, at 10:00 a.m., I noticed his breathing was rapid and shallow. We had visited the park three days prior, and I assumed the grass had triggered his allergies. The veterinarian in our new state prescribed him medication and instructed me to give him steam to ease his breathing. For three nights, with my head resting against my bed's frame and mattress, I sat on the floor and cradled Chez in my arms so he could inhale the humidifier's warm steam and sleep. I would make any sacrifice required to ensure Chez was healthy and happy. In our life together, we experienced two luxated patella surgeries, one cranial cruciate ligament rupture (CCLR) repair (equivalent to an ACL in humans), several physical therapy sessions, and an organic food diet. But, on March 9, my efforts were beyond my human ability and were not enough.

At 10:00 a.m., as Chez sat in his downstairs bed with unrhythmic breathing, I saw sadness in his eyes. I retrieved my phone and recorded Chez's breathing to email to Dr. Tanner, Chez's long-term veterinarian, because I wanted a second opinion to the one I had received from the veterinarian in our new state. But as I watched Chez, I knew I could not wait for a response from Dr. Tanner. I scooped him into my arms, jumped in my vehicle, and quickly drove to the veterinarian's office. I arrived at the office, and unexpectedly, their chief of staff was present. The chief of staff and I had developed a respectful doctor-patient relationship after having a "meeting of the minds," during which I had informed her that Chez was not the average dog, and that I expected her to be accurate with her diagnosis of issues and suggested treatments. That conversation arose from a prior misdiagnosis. She removed Chez from his travel bag and vanished into the back of the clinic, but she quickly reappeared and said that Chez needed oxygen because she believed the issue was with his heart. My eyes widened and my mind raced. What was happening? He'd just had his annual physical and dental cleaning two months prior, and there had been no mention of a heart issue. As I sat perplexed, she sprang into action and called the animal emergency hospital. She instructed me to run outside to retrieve my vehicle, and as the nurse followed close behind her, she ran to meet me at the front of the clinic. She placed Chez on the front seat and said, "Drive! Drive! They are waiting for you. I hope you make it."

Chez's breathing became more labored as I weaved through traffic and ran traffic lights. I moved him from the passenger seat onto my lap as I sped through traffic and merged onto the highway. I sang to him and talked loudly to keep him awake. I told him to hang on because I was going to make him feel better. I maintained that promise to him for fourteen years, and this time would be no different. "Stay with me, Chez! Stay with Mommy!" I prayed loudly, "God, protect Chez. Don't take him from me!"

We arrived at the animal emergency hospital. With Chez cradled in my arms, I ran inside.

"Is that Chez?" asked the nurse.

"Yes," I replied.

She grabbed him from my arms and raced to the back of the hospital to place Chez in an oxygen cage.

"We have a stat!" I heard the nurse yell.

From the moment Chez was taken from my arms, time seemed to have slowed. I was ushered to a small waiting room, where I sat in silence. Eventually, the emergency room doctor entered the room.

"Miss Smith, I am Doctor Ross. Chez is in the oxygen cage and his breathing is stable. But, Miss Smith, I believe it is his heart," he said.

"How?" I asked.

Dr. Ross could not be certain, but was sure it was Chez's heart.

He continued, "It could be his lungs, an infection, or his heart, but I need to obtain X-rays to be certain. And because he needs the oxygen crate to stabilize his breathing, Miss Smith, I think it is his heart."

"I want to see him," I said, still in disbelief.

Dr. Ross escorted me to the operating room where Chez lay on his side on a metal table, with an oxygen mask covering his mouth and nostrils.

"We removed him from the oxygen cage to get X-rays," the doctor explained. "But we have to put him back because he isn't breathing sufficiently on his own, and that is not good."

"Can he hear me?" I asked.

"Yes," he replied.

"Chez. Chez. It's Mommy. Fight for Mommy, Chez. You gotta fight. Stay with me," I pleaded.

"Stay with us, Chez," Dr. Ross and the nurse echoed.

At that moment, Chez took a huge breath, and his eyes widened. I panicked.

"What is happening?" I asked.

"His body isn't holding on," Dr. Ross said. "Do you want me to intubate him?" he asked.

"What is that?!" I asked.

"It is where we insert a very small tube into his airway. It will not hurt him," Dr. Ross explained.

"Yes! Intubate him. Save him," I cried.

The nurse's hand grasped my arm, and she escorted me back to the waiting room. The minutes slowed to a crawl. At 1:00 p.m., Dr. Ross entered the waiting room with an update and a request.

"Miss Smith, Chez is not stabilizing. He went into respiratory arrest. We are now doing CPR. Do you want us to continue?"

"Yes!" I replied, while my thoughts screamed, *do not return to speak with me. Stay in the room with Chez and save him!*

Time slowed to a crawl. I looked up at the clock on the wall. 1:15 p.m. The minute hand ticked, and Dr. Ross reappeared in the patient room where I sat.

His next sentence began with a heavy sigh, and he said, "Miss Smith, I am sorry, but Chez is gone. His little body just couldn't hang on."

I sat stunned and completely numb to his words. I couldn't process what he had just said.

"Miss Smith, is there someone I can call for you?" he continued.

There was a ringing in my ears. I sucked in the little breath I had because it felt as if a plastic bag covered my face. Without warning, a cry traveled from the depths of my soul and dispensed with such force that Dr. Ross rocked backward onto the heels of his feet. Instantly, my heart was ripped away from me, and left an unapologetic void. My head shook from side to side as I repeated, "No, no, no. Oh, God no!" "Bring him to me," I sobbed.

"Yes, ma'am," he said.

Dr. Ross returned holding Chez in his arms, wrapped in a tan towel. He gently placed his small, still warm body in my arms and stepped back. Seated, I pulled Chez close to my chest as I sobbed. His body was so warm and still. His eyes were open. For the first time, I was holding my heart outside of my body. Between sobs, I whispered to Chez, "Why did you have to leave me?" I looked up at Dr. Ross. "I've read that a person can still hear immediately after they die, do you think Chez can hear me?" I asked.

"I believe so," he replied.

"Chez, Mommy loves you. Mommy loves you."

I rocked him in my arms until Dr. Ross asked, "May I take him?" I reluctantly nodded approval. He extended his reach toward me and removed him from my arms. Picking up Chez's blanket, which was draped in my lap, I covered my face with it and wailed. "We will call the funeral home. Is that OK with you?" he asked.

I sobbed and nodded approval.

"Miss Smith, are you sure there isn't someone I can call for you? We can call a driver if you cannot drive home."

I shook my head no. I could not comprehend what had happened. Chez and I had been at the park on Sunday, and by Wednesday he was gone.

Disoriented, I rose from the chair and opened the waiting room door. I looked down the emergency hospital's hallway. What was once a short hallway now appeared endless. Slowly, I made the walk to the reception desk. My thoughts raced. Was the staff aware that Chez had died? I didn't know. I couldn't read their faces. My eyes were swollen, and my face was tearstained.

"Miss Smith, an email with Chez's vet records arrived," said a female staffer.

She doesn't know, I thought.

"I don't need them now," I said.

Her gaze traveled away from her computer screen until it met mine. "Oh, I am sorry," she said. She handed me a payment receipt. "If you need us, please call."

I loosely held the receipt, while attempting to process the reason I was not leaving with Chez. With shallow breaths, dazed and with my mouth agape, I turned and stumbled out of the animal hospital without Chez. *What had just happened? Oh, God, what had happened?* After Chez and I had been together for fourteen years, he had finally crossed the rainbow bridge.

The following days and weeks were filled with flowers, cards, and gifts from those who had loved little Chez. An outside observer would have assumed a human being had died. To me, a person, my family member had died. My housekeeper and I visited Chez at the pet crematory for a private viewing. The staff placed Chez's little body on a bed with his head resting on a pillow. He looked so peaceful. I wept.

However, what others could not see was the deep sadness that had taken residence within me. I grappled with the events of March 9, and I tried to navigate life without him. His toys, food and water bowls, blankets, beds, treats, and hygiene products were in their proper places, yet Chez was not present. I attended a pet grief counseling session, but the session was not effective because nobody could explain the reason for the void that I felt. As such, I sought answers outside of and against my spiritual background, and I contacted a pet medium. The conversation with the pet medium did not provide answers either.

For months, I replayed the events of my last day with Chez. I wondered what I could have done differently or what I should have noticed sooner. The blame game was not healthy for me, nor is it for you. To get through my days and months of grief, I wrote letters to him, journaled our memories, and authored poems. It is within the pages of this journal and memory book that I will share some of my healing journey as I help you with your path to healing.

Begin your journey with truly believing that you were a great caretaker of your dog. However, your beloved dog has crossed the rainbow bridge, and there was nothing that you could have done differently to change the trajectory of their destination. It was in God's plan, and it was your beloved fur baby's time.

> There was nothing more that you could have done. You were a great parent to Chez. Everything in life happens for a reason.
> —Dr. Kerrwen Tanner, DVM

The Journey

Beginning Your Journey to Moving beyond the Rainbow Bridge

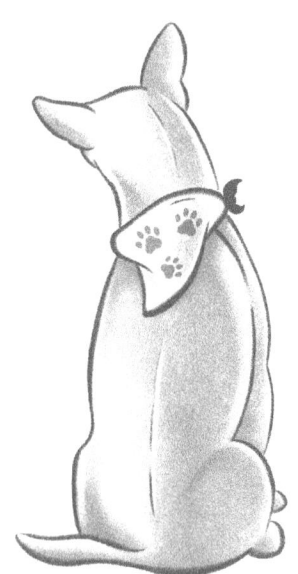

OUR EXPERIENCES OF HOW OUR dogs have crossed the rainbow bridge may differ. As dog owners, one emotion we share is the unfathomed pain our dog's departure leaves with us. We grieve, process, and uniquely determine how to move beyond that period of time. As such, I have constructed the following pages of this guided book, comprised of inspirational poems, quotes, writings, and guided journal prompts with you in mind. Because we experience and process grief differently, this journal is meant to assist with your healing journey. At the conclusion of the six months, you may not be free of your grief because you will always miss your fur baby. Likewise, being "free" should not be the goal; rather, the goal should be for you to be able to think of and talk about your beloved dog from a cheerful space. I encourage you to be active in your grief process. Be gentle with yourself, and give yourself grace. You did not lose just a dog; you have lost your family, and you deserve to grieve and work through the process. May the memories, poems, and letters make you laugh, cry, and encourage you to write your own memories about the joy that your beloved dog brought to your life and find peace to move beyond the rainbow bridge.

Dogs impart a special love which renews daily. A dog's love does not keep a record of how we treat them on our bad days. They are always cheerful to see us. They endure life with us. They never leave our side. And they thank us for loving them. A dog's love is a reflection of a perfect love. When our beloved dog departs this life, their absence is deafening and leaves a void that cannot be explained. What do you do when they cross the rainbow bridge?

The poem, *The Rainbow Bridge*, written by an unknown author, is a beautiful story about how your pet transitions to the afterlife where their health is restored, their energy is high, they play with all animals, and they see your loved ones who have departed before you, but they always miss someone special. That special someone is you. When you leave this life, their bright light knows it, and they excitedly race back to your arms and reunite with you for eternity. Until that day arrives, let's begin your healing journey with a letter to your fur baby and best friend.

> Love is patient and kind. Love is not jealous or boastful or proud or rude. It does not demand its own way. It is not irritable, and it keeps no record of being wronged.
> —1 Corinthians 13:4–5 (NLT)

> Love never gives up, never loses faith, is always hopeful, and endures through every circumstance.
> —1 Corinthians 13:7 (NLT)

Pictures are worth a thousand words…
Place photos of your beloved dog with you and those who loved them here.

A Letter to My Best Friend

The Day You Crossed the Rainbow Bridge

Date:_____

Dear _____,
       (dog's name)

_____
_____
_____
_____
_____
_____
_____

Love, _____

First Month

The journey to healing begins, one month at a time.

THIS MONTH IS VERY DIFFICULT because life as you knew it, with your faithful friend and companion, has changed. Whether you helped your fur baby cross the rainbow bridge or it happened unexpectedly, you may wrestle with your thoughts amid tears and sadness. You are not alone. I wrote letters on behalf of Chez to the people who had cared for Chez during his life. Showing gratitude is healing.

Who would you write a letter to thank them on behalf of your beloved dog? On the following page, the first exercise is for you to write a letter to someone whom you or your fur baby would thank for their care or the love they showed your beloved dog in their life. I began this chapter with a lettered poem to Dr. Tanner from Chez.

>He heals the brokenhearted and bandages their wounds.
>—Psalms 147:3 (NLT)

THANK YOU FOR THE YEARS

To: Dr. Kerrwen Tanner, DVM
On behalf of: Chez Smith

Thank you for taking care of me with such knowledge,
skill and without fear.
You did your job so well with me,
no one could guess I was well beyond my years.
You knew my personality because I would peek at you from my crate,
and give one miniature bark to keep you and the staff awake.
You would tell me hello because that was all I needed to hear,
then I allowed you to continue caring for other animals as you did for me
throughout my years.
My unexpected, swift departure brought my mom to tears.
I left the world as I entered,
as a reserved Yorkshire terrier, who was calm and cool as can be.
I don't have much more to say,
which is typical for me.
I wanted to make sure you knew my gratitude
for all the years you took care of me.

Chez Smith
11/19/2008–03/9/2022

First Month

Let's begin this month of your healing journey by thanking one person on behalf of _____. You may write a letter, poem, or song. Be creative.
   (dog's name)

Who would my fur baby thank for their care? Was it a doctor, family member, friend?

*Date:*_____

_____
_____
_____
_____
_____
_____
_____
_____
_____
_____
_____
_____
_____
_____
_____
_____
_____
_____

NOISY SILENCE

You had me at hello and again at goodbye.
I never thought about the day,
your absence would make me cry.
I walk in the house and run upstairs,
only to be reminded that you are no longer there.
Your bed sits atop my bed. Your blanket too.
I truly do not know what to do without you.
The house is extra quiet now,
although it was never loud.
Yet something about your missing presence
brings an extra hushed cloud.
I try to eat and sleep. It is so hard to do.
I really…truly…and terribly miss you.

The first month without your fur baby is difficult because the silence of their absence is loud. Take a moment to write about your new silence and how it makes you feel.

I notice your absence when…

Date: _____

What noises did your fur baby make that you no longer hear?

My life has changed because there are certain noises that I no longer hear…

*Date:*_____

_____
_____
_____
_____
_____
_____
_____
_____
_____
_____
_____
_____
_____
_____
_____
_____
_____
_____
_____

Days after Chez died, I wanted to understand the reason I was not prepared for his rapid decline. A conversation with a friend revealed that God had actually prepared me. Our conversation went like this:

PREPARING ME

He said:
You are more spiritual than I am,
but I know this was God's plan.
You did everything you could do.
Yet, God had a plan too.

I said:
I know God has plans.
I wish He would have given me time to prepare.
To know this was coming,
I could have avoided such despair.
I spent two nights holding him,
in front of warm steam to breathe.
I sat on the floor, legs crossed, circulation stopped,
which caused my feet to fall asleep.
My head rested against the bed, eyes closed,
but wide awake, I needed to remain alert for his little sake.

His reply:
You weren't paying attention.
You had something else on your mind.
God was preparing you for his departure during that time.
The nights you stayed awake,
holding him in your arms,
That was the time God gave you,
so you wouldn't be alarmed.
This is rather easy to see.
Even though you are more spiritual than me.

I replied:
I didn't think God was preparing me.
At least not in that way.
Because I was doing everything to make him better;
I wanted him to stay.
Holding him in my arms all night,
praying he would be alright.
Preoccupied? Perhaps. I guess you are right.
God was preparing me, which I did not see.
Now He is using you to tell me,
A man who is less spiritual than me.

"My thoughts are nothing like your thoughts," says the Lord. "And my ways are far beyond anything you could imagine."
—Isaiah 55:8 (NLT)

You may feel blindsided by your dog's departure, or you may wonder if you made the correct decision to help them cross over. Regardless, their death prompts thoughts about the events leading to their last days, and you may wonder if any signs had been overlooked. Think about the last days and moments. Did you feel prepared for your beloved fur baby's departure?

What were the last moments that I spent with my dog?

*Date:*_____

First Month

There will be times out of the day that are difficult because you had a routine with
_____. Take a moment to explore this area.

   (dog's name)

The most difficult time of the day for me is…

*Date:*_____

_____

_____

_____

_____

_____

_____

_____

_____

_____

_____

_____

_____

_____

_____

_____

_____

Second Month

ONE THING IS CERTAIN, WHILE we *think* we are training our amazing dogs, they are actually training us. Our dogs train us to feed them at certain hours, walk them, play with them, to listen, and the list continues. It is comical to think about how well our dogs train us to be all that they need us to be for them, and to be better humans.

The second month is to help you shift to memorable moments when your beloved dog amazed you. Write about the moments when you thought you were training them, and they were actually training you.

> The Lord is merciful and compassionate, slow to get angry and filled with unfailing love. The Lord is good to everyone. He showers compassion on all his creation.
> —Psalms 145:8–9 (NLT)

TRAINED

It's a strange feeling to not have to rush home to you.
I trained you well to wait for me.
But if I was a little too late,
you would wet the bed in your crate or defecate.
That was how you showed me you were upset.
I guess I was the one being trained.
I would look at my watch and timed my return just right,
to rush back home to you.
You had feelings and personality and you let me know.
Your displeasure with my delayed returns
were met with promises from me to not do it again.
But now, I don't have to rush home,
and I don't know what to do.
You trained me well, can't you tell?
I am missing you.

Second Month

Remember some of the good times with _____. How did your beloved dog train you?   *(dog's name)*

My fur baby trained me to…

*Date:*_____

How did you know that your fur baby was teaching you to be a better human?

I became a better person when/because…

*Date:*_____

A SHARED MEMORY
Hold My Sneeze, Please!

I did not realize that I sneezed loudly, as if I were in pain, until Chez let me know. When Chez was around three years old, he would race to where I stood, barking uncontrollably when I sneezed. My sneezes felt as if my membrane was ejecting out of my head; however, I didn't realize that it sounded as such.

Each time I sneezed, I would reassure Chez that I was OK. "I'm OK, Chez. I'm OK. Mommy's OK," I would tell him. After the third reassurance, he would settle and cautiously watch me with a hint distrust. Nevertheless, his little cropped tail would rapidly wiggle from side to side in anticipation of another sneeze. When he felt assured that another sneeze would not emerge, he would calmly walk away. Chez trained me to stifle my sneezes, and I often found myself laughing at my attempts to contain sneezes to the lowest decibel. The times I didn't contain my sneeze, Chez would go into full barking action.

Chez is gone now, and I still notice myself holding my sneezes. After almost fifteen years, I admit that he trained me pretty well.

Chez was truly amazing at teaching lessons, which I incorporated and practiced in my interactions with people. As such, I became conscious about the impact that my words have on others. For example, when I conversed with others and communicated my thoughts, I delivered statements without regard to the *impact* that my words had on the listener. Although my communications never arose from ill intent, I did not understand that there may have been an issue. However, Chez taught me that the impact of my words matter, and he taught me to observe the facial expressions of the listener because nonverbal expressions communicate just as loudly as words. Thank you, Chez.

What characteristics or habits have you changed because of your fur baby?

I am more _____ and _____ toward others or myself because…

Date:_____

TODAY, I CRIED

You have been gone two months,
and three weeks.
I stopped crying at two months,
and began smiling at your memories.
I could look at your pictures,
and smile without tears.
Two months,
and three weeks, but today…
I cried.

We are imperfect humans, and therefore, we make mistakes. However, your fur baby had a way of showing their displeasure with your bad behavior.

I knew when you were not pleased with my actions because…

*Date:*_____

_____
_____
_____
_____
_____
_____
_____
_____
_____
_____
_____
_____
_____
_____
_____
_____
_____

What do you do better because of your fur family member?

You taught me to be better at…

*Date:*_____

Writing memories about your dog can make you laugh uncontrollably. What is a memory that you shared with your fur baby?

You always made me laugh when…

*Date:*_____

Second Month

Write a memory that makes you smile or laugh aloud to yourself when you think of your beloved dog.

I laugh when I think about…

*Date:*_____

Third Month

I AM SO PLEASED THAT YOU are working through this process because the third month is still a difficult month. But your dedication to the process has enabled you to find your voice to be creative and pen your thoughts, tears, and last words to your fur baby. This month, you will journal about your dog's character, their ability to love you beyond yourself, and how it made you feel.

When we are truly loved, we feel it. Dogs love us beyond our own expectations, and we feel their love deep within our souls. Let's keep going into month three and explore our creativity with great memories.

A DOG'S ESSENCE

A dog will…
Look past your flaws
Celebrate your wins
Protect your safety
Sit quietly with you in solitude
Dance at your smile
Console your sadness
Forget your indiscretions, and
Forgive your faults.

A dog will…
Remind you to keep going
Delight in your presence
Comfort your soul
Give you your why
Relish in your time
Lie beside you in illness
Overlook your shortcomings, and
Love you until they die.
It is no wonder it is said,
that dogs are treated better than humans.
It is because a dog's love
extends beyond the imagination of man.

How do you feel when you are loved despite your flaws and without any expectation?

You showed me that you loved me beyond my expectations when…

Date: _____

There are days when you just do not feel your best; however, your fur baby always brought a ray of sunshine to your day. When have you felt down and your beloved dog made you feel better or made your day brighter?

You cheered me up when…

*Date:*_____

Third Month

Your fur baby's personality was uniquely their own, which made you smile and have belly laughs. How did your fur baby show their personality?

You showed me your personality when…

*Date:*_____

FIRST QUARTER

Three months since you have been gone,
yet your memory lives on.
Today,
I thought about how you loved to sit in front of the fire.
You would only walk away for a drink of water,
and return to your spot.
You were my Yorkie log during the winter.
Three months since you have been gone,
it really isn't that long.
Time passes slower,
a teardrop rolls down my cheek.
Your beds are still in their respective places,
and so is your crate.
My heart still aches.

There will be times when something triggers you to think of your fur baby. What has reminded you of them?

Today, I thought of you…

*Date:*_____

I smile more because…

*Date:*_____

Fourth Month

I BELIEVE THAT DOGS ARE SOME of the most special animals that God created. There is something special about the nature of a dog that cannot be duplicated. Dogs are little fur humans who train us to love with all that we have, give selflessly, forgive quickly, laugh loudly, and walk away from people who may not be kind to us.

Dogs teach us these lessons without words; therefore, we are required to pay attention to them to understand them. They require us to focus on them and learn who they are; they master these lessons without force or demands. When we are quiet, watch, and listen to our beloved dogs, we learn lessons that we would otherwise overlook. Use the fourth month to remember and write about how special your dog was to you and others, and the lessons they taught you.

> Keep watch and pray, so that you will not give in to temptation. For the spirit is willing, but the body is weak.
> —Matthew 26:41 (NLT)

SOMETHING SPECIAL

I knew you were special.
You weren't yet four months,
three and a half to be exact.
I left you at the bottom of the stairs,
and told you I would be right back.
Your legs were so tiny,
no longer than the eraser on the end of a pencil.
You watched me ascend to the top.
Waiting for my return—or so I thought.
I walked into the hallway and looked down.
How did you get up here?
You climbed so fast and without a sound.
You sat staring back at me.
I knew you were something special.

Your righteousness is like the mighty mountains, your justice like the ocean depths. You care for people and animals alike, O LORD.
—Psalms 36:6 (NLT)

Fourth Month

When did you know that _____ was a special dog, created just for you?
                      (dog's name)

I knew you were special when…

Date:_____

Insert photos and items from special moments.

Fourth Month 53

There were others who were impacted positively by your loving dog. How did your fur baby impact the lives of others?

I remember how you impacted…

*Date:*_____

_____
_____
_____
_____
_____
_____
_____
_____
_____
_____
_____
_____
_____
_____
_____
_____
_____

Fifth Month

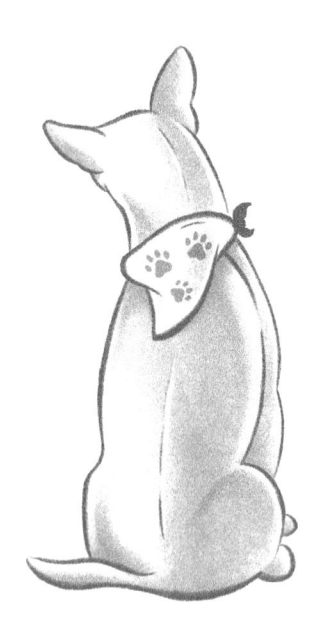

THE FIFTH MONTH CAN FEEL like the first month because there may be an event or activity that reminds you of how important your loving dog was in your life. For me, the event that made Chez's absence feel like the first month was traveling out of state for the first time since his death. Chez was my little road warrior. His seat in the truck was in the back, on the passenger side. While driving, I would often glance in the back to see what he was doing as we drove on our trips. In my fifth month, my glance to the back seat was met with only his bedding in his place because he was no longer there. Let's work through the fifth month of healing.

THE LONGEST DRIVE HOME

The longest and hardest drive home
is the one without you.
When I glance in the car's back seat,
you are not there.
The absence of your presence is quiet.
I have no one to sing to on this five-hour drive.
My fuel stops won't include your potty breaks,
or asking you to wait as I refresh your water bowl.
The longest and hardest drive home
is the one without you,
because I'll be driving home alone.

Fifth Month 57

For this entry, it may be difficult, but you can do it. In what ways are you missing _____?

(dog's name)

Today, I really miss you because…

*Date:*_____

_____
_____
_____
_____
_____
_____
_____
_____
_____
_____
_____
_____
_____
_____
_____

There will be days when certain activities will trigger memories of your fur baby. What is your new normal?

Today is when we would_____, and now I do it without you.

Date:_____

ETERNAL HOPE

Do you miss me as I miss you?
Do you know I am not with you?
I whisper to you, hoping you will hear me.
I hope Heaven greeted you with open arms,
and you are being treated well.
You weren't aggressive, but timid and shy.
I pray you are strong and healthy
in that heavenly sky.
I always wanted the best for you.
I miss you.

The Lord is close to the brokenhearted; he rescues those whose spirits are crushed.
—Psalms 34:18 (NLT)

Positive memories and hopes help to heal the heart. What is a positive wish that you have about your beloved dog, _____?
(dog's name)

I hope that you are happy and healthy because…

Date:_____

DETERMINATION

When Chez was three months old, his little legs eagerly carried him throughout my townhome. He followed me everywhere I walked. It was so adorable to look behind me and see his little body wobbling to keep up. The only area of the home where he could not follow me was to the upstairs bedrooms. So he would follow me to the foyer and wait for me to return downstairs. I always told Chez that I would return quickly. "I'll be right back, OK? I will be right back." Chez sat and waited at the bottom of the staircase because he trusted me—until the day he did not wait for my return.

The day began as normal. Chez followed me throughout the townhome, like my shadow. We arrived in the foyer, at the foot of the staircase. As customary, I told Chez to wait, and that I would be right back. I walked upstairs to my bedroom suite. As I exited my bedroom to descend downstairs, I looked down, and to my surprise, there sat little Chez in the hallway. "How did you get up here?" I asked. Chez didn't respond or move. Rather, he sat unbothered, and his mahogany-brown eyes stared back at me. "I didn't hear you climb the stairs," I continued. I spoke to him as if he was going to respond. He remained still and quiet. I picked him up with a mix of giddiness and fear. I was giddy because he had just amazed me. I felt fear because, being so small, he could have hurt himself climbing the large steps. But, in that moment, Chez showed me he was determined, and his determination played throughout his life.

Your fur baby had talents unlike any other dog, and it was what made them so unique. What made your dog's personality unique?

I saw your unique personality when…

*Date:*_____

Fifth Month

I saw your determination and resilience when…

*Date:*_____

TOO INTELLIGENT FOR ME

In October 2009, Chez and I relocated to a new state. Chez was almost one year old. A couple of months into living in our new city, I had the genius idea to adopt another puppy. I thought another dog would give Chez a playmate and decrease his attachment to me. I immediately learned that two dogs meant two dogs were attached to me. Anyway, I was at the local pet store, and it was adoption day. I saw the most adorable and gentle-spirited female beagle-and-Yorkie mixed puppy. She was a few weeks old and an absolute doll. I adopted her and named her Jade. I brought Jade home, and Chez immediately began to check her out. At one year old, Chez tried to show the new puppy that he was the alpha pup. I also thought that I probably had made a wrong decision in acquiring a nine-week-old puppy, and within twenty-four hours, I returned Jade to the adoption shelter. I was sad to return Jade, but I knew it was the best decision. Unsurprisingly, Jade was rehomed to a new family within twenty-four hours of her return. However, the day before I took Jade back to the shelter, Chez demonstrated that he was highly intelligent and intuitive.

The day after I brought Jade home, I placed her in Chez's crate while I showered. As I dressed, after my shower, Chez sat in my room with me. I looked at him and said, "Chez, go check on Jade." Seated, Chez blankly stared at me. "Chez, go check on Jade for me," I repeated. Chez stood, walked out of my room and toward the guest room, and stood at the entrance to the guest room. My eyes followed him as he peered into his crate where Jade rested. Chez walked back to my room and looked at me as if to say, "She is fine." Yet I still spoke to him. "Thank you. Is Jade OK?" I asked. Chez sat down in response to my question. Jade was OK. That day, Chez taught me that he understood me and was highly intelligent.

Fifth Month

When did you realize _____ was intelligent or intuitive?
                        (dog's name)

I knew you were a very smart dog when…

*Date:*_____

I knew you were intuitive because…

*Date:*_____

Sixth Month

IT HAS BEEN SIX MONTHS, and the days are brighter for some, while others need more time. You have made it this far in your healing journey, and as you continue to do the work, your fur baby's memories will bring you more laughter than tears. This process takes time. Give yourself grace.

For the sixth month, I encourage you to write about your days during this month and how moving forward looks for you. This process may be long or short, but it is your new normal. I have included blank pages for you to be creative because your healing journey is unique to you and does not end at the sixth month. Your beloved dog will always be in your heart. Use this journal to keep your memory of them, and your memories with them, alive.

When was my first day that I awoke without a tearstained face or pillow?

*Date:*_____

*Dear*_____,
    (dog's name)

Write about the goal you set for yourself and achieved today.

How would my fur baby react to my accomplishment or achievement?

*Date:*_____

*Dear*_____,
    (dog's name)

_____
_____
_____
_____
_____
_____
_____
_____
_____
_____
_____
_____
_____
_____

Tell your dog how much they are missed.

What other person or people will miss my dog?

*Date:*_____

*Dear*_____,
      (dog's name)

_____
_____
_____
_____
_____
_____
_____
_____
_____
_____
_____
_____
_____
_____
_____
_____

Write about the steps or plans you made for your dog, to ensure they were always cared for.

*Date:*_____

Sixth Month

If your dog had fur friends or siblings that they left on this side of the rainbow bridge, then take a moment to write about their fur friends' or siblings' feelings and the changes you've noticed.

Example: _____ sleeps in your bed every day now to feel close to you.

Date:_____

_____
_____
_____
_____
_____
_____
_____
_____
_____
_____
_____
_____
_____
_____
_____
_____
_____
_____

Sixth Month

Take time to write about how you feel when you see your dog's toys on the floor in your home.

When I see your toys, I feel…

Date:_____

How do you feel when you see your beloved dog's food bowl, blanket, or bed?

When I see your food bowl and bed, I feel…

*Date:*_____

Sixth Month

People may ask if you will get another dog because they want to be helpful in your healing journey. However, only you know when—and if—that will happen. Take a moment to write to your dog about your feelings when you are asked about bringing another dog home.

When I am asked if I will get another dog, I think/feel…

*Date:*_____

*Dear*_____,
    (dog's name)

_____

_____

_____

_____

_____

_____

_____

_____

_____

_____

_____

_____

_____

_____

LETTER TO CHEZ

Writing letters to Chez was healing for me because there was so much to say to him.

Dear Chez,

Last week I took my first trip out of the country since you left. I traveled to Milan and Venice, and it felt strange because I returned from this trip and did not drive to pick you up from boarding. It felt really unnatural, and I was sad because I liked asking you if you missed me and giving you a new toy to show you that I thought of you while I was away. Things are truly different without you. Not to mention, it is very quiet.

During my trip, I saw so many dogs with their owners. It was heartbreaking because this was the first trip that I did not search for a gift for you. I wore your ashes in a chain every day and everywhere I went. I hope you felt that you were with me. I didn't cry while I was in Italy, but you were on my mind each day. Taking care of you was the hardest and most rewarding assignment that I have ever had in my life. I hope that you are proud of how I cared for you. I miss you.

Love,
Mommy

Write a letter to your fur baby.

Is there anything new that I want to tell my fur baby? What are my emotions about their absence at six months?

*Date:*_____

*Dear*_____,
      (dog's name)

_____

_____

_____

_____

_____

_____

_____

_____

_____

_____

_____

_____

Love,
_____

Sixth Month

At six months, what trips have you taken without your beloved dog or what activities have you participated in?

I took a trip (local, stateside, or abroad) to_____ and I felt…

Date:_____

_____
_____
_____
_____
_____
_____
_____
_____
_____
_____
_____
_____
_____
_____
_____
_____
_____

Sixth Month

How are your travel or local trips to certain places different now?

It feels different to not travel to _____(place or retailer) because I always went for you…

Date:_____

TIME

I saw time fall upon you…
Your walk was a little slower.
Your head hung a bit lower.
You sped up when I cheered you on,
but it wasn't at your two-year-old speed.
Your quick pace never lasted very long.

I saw time fall upon you…
I believe God spared my heart
because He did not turn your coat gray.
Rather, He placed a silver hair here and there.
Made them appear like stowaways.

I saw time fall upon you…
I could feel it in my soul.
I cringed at the words from others, "Chez is getting old."

Time was upon you…
When I began to carry you up the stairs.
At first I figured you were being stubborn,
but realized the energy was just not there.

Time was upon you…
You'd sleep more than you were awake.
I began placing my hand on your belly
just to make sure I could feel the breaths you take.

Time was upon you…
Each day I awoke and saw you alive.
I exhaled a sigh of relief,
and thanked God I could look into your eyes.

Sixth Month

Time was upon you…
Your bladder didn't hold as well.
So, I permanently kept potty pads
in your beds so you wouldn't feel any shame.

Time was upon you…
The prescription food, you no longer liked.
So I boiled rice, chicken, and carrots
with yogurt—a bland diet to tickle your appetite.

Time was upon me…
I refused to believe that you
and I had been together almost fifteen years,
I still had more for you to see.

Time was upon me…
Because my gut had me wonder each night
if that would be the last night I'd see you.
So, I kissed the top of your head and told you I loved you.

Time was upon us…
The clock stopped ticking.
Finally, time was here.

What changes did you see in your fur baby as they grew from a puppy to a senior dog?

As you grew from a puppy, the changes I saw…

Date:_____

Create, Collage, Collaborate

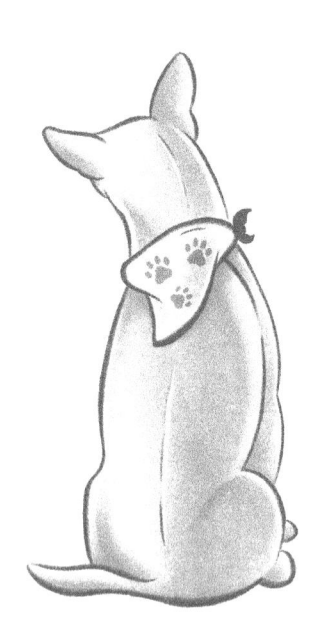

USE THE FOLLOWING PAGES TO AFFIX more photos of your fur baby, draw, or write about the memories that bring you joy.

Your Healing Continues

GRIEF HAS NO TIME LIMIT or deadline. However, grief finds its exit when healing enters. Writing your stories, memories, poems, and journal entries is a healthy and positive way to remember your dog. Your dog was uniquely created to love you and usher moments into your life that were designed only for you to experience.

My goal in this journal was to share some of the magical moments that Chez brought to my life, to feel the love he gave me and the love I returned to him, while guiding you through your healing journey as you recount your dog's memories, life lessons, love, laughter, and even the sadness that you experienced.

Thank you for choosing to take your first six months of your healing journey within the pages of this journal.

The following pages are for you to draft, draw, and photo collage as you desire because your dog crossed the rainbow bridge. As painful as it was to lose your fur baby, your journey to healing now requires you to *move beyond the rainbow bridge*.

Love, light, and laughter,

Julieta L. Smith

Tears cleanse the soul to remind you that you will smile again.
—Anonymous

Your Healing Continues

Your Healing Continues

Your Healing Continues

Printed in the USA
CPSIA information can be obtained
at www.ICGtesting.com
JSHW070820251123
52375JS00012B/16